Lewis H. Meader

The Council of Censors

Lewis H. Meader

The Council of Censors

ISBN/EAN: 9783337300906

Printed in Europe, USA, Canada, Australia, Japan

Cover: Foto ©Andreas Hilbeck / pixelio.de

More available books at **www.hansebooks.com**

Papers from the Historical Seminary
of Brown University

Edited by J. FRANKLIN JAMESON, Ph. D., LL. D., Professor of History

X

THE COUNCIL OF CENSORS

BY

LEWIS HAMILTON MEADER, A. M.

REPRINTED FROM THE
PENNSYLVANIA MAGAZINE OF HISTORY AND BIOGRAPHY
AND FROM THE
PROCEEDINGS OF THE VERMONT HISTORICAL SOCIETY

PROVIDENCE
1899

Reprinted from THE PENNSYLVANIA MAGAZINE OF HISTORY AND
BIOGRAPHY, *October, 1898.*

THE COUNCIL OF CENSORS.

I. INTRODUCTORY.

In 1776 a Constitutional Convention met in Philadelphia
and framed a constitution for Pennsylvania which contained
the following provision for its change or amendment:[1]

"Sect. 47. In order that the freedom of the commonwealth may be
preserved inviolate forever, there shall be chosen by ballot by the freemen in each city and county respectively, on the second Tuesday in
October, in the year one thousand seven hundred and eighty-three, and
on the second Tuesday in October in every seventh year thereafter, two
persons in each city and county of this state, to be called THE COUNCIL
OF CENSORS; who shall meet together on the second Monday of November next ensuing their election; the majority of whom shall be a
quorum in every case, except as to calling a convention, in which two
thirds of the whole number elected shall agree: And whose duty it shall
be to enquire whether the constitution has been preserved inviolate in
every part; and whether the legislative and executive branches of government have performed their duty as guardians of the people, or assumed to themselves, or exercised other or greater powers than they are
intitled to by the constitution: They are also to enquire whether the
public taxes have been justly laid and collected in all parts of this commonwealth, in what manner the public monies have been disposed of,
and whether the laws have been duly executed. For these purposes they
shall have power to send for persons, papers, and records; they shall
have authority to pass public censures, to order impeachments, and to
recommend to the legislature the repealing of such laws as appear to
them to have been enacted contrary to the principles of the constitution. These powers they shall continue to have, for and during the
space of one year from the day of their election and no longer: The
said council of censors shall also have power to call a convention,

[1] Poore, "Charters and Constitutions," Vol. II. p. 1548.

to meet within two years after their sitting, if there appear to them an absolute necessity of amending any article of the constitution which may be defective, explaining such as may be thought not clearly expressed, and of adding such as are necessary for the preservation of the rights and happiness of the people : But the articles to be amended, and the amendments proposed, and such articles as are proposed to be added or abolished, shall be promulgated at least six months before the day appointed for the election of such convention, for the previous consideration of the people, that they may have an opportunity of instructing their delegates on the subject." [1]

This constitution vested the supreme executive power in a president and council, the supreme legislative power in a House of Representatives of the freemen of the Commonwealth or State of Pennsylvania, but it recognized no separate body invested with supreme judicial power.

This so-called Council of Censors constituted the recognized legal check on the executive and legislative branches of the government, and in it alone was vested the means whereby the constitution could be amended or altered.

This council was to be elected once in seven years by the people, each county and city to be represented by two councillors; it was to exist and have power one year from the date of its election, and no longer. It was a feature of the constitution of Pennsylvania from 1776 to 1790, and of that of Vermont from 1777 to 1869.

It is the purpose of this inquiry to trace the growth, in Pennsylvania and elsewhere, of this device for preserving and revising constitutional provisions, and to note the causes which have led to its being superseded and finally driven from the field.

II. Censors in Europe.

The name, Council of Censors, leads one to look for a model in the government of Rome, and to examine this to detect points of similarity and contrast; for one might reasonably conjecture that when a people in a given in-

---

[1] "The Proceedings relative to calling the Conventions of 1776 and 1790, the Minutes of the Convention . . . and of the Council of Censors," Harrisburg, 1825.

stance were about to frame a constitution over which the people should have control, the most prominent examples of history would be studied to the end that their excellencies might be imitated and their errors and weaknesses avoided. This hypothesis seems the more reasonable when one considers that the models of Greece and Rome, together with those of Rousseau and other theorists, were the only prominent ones, and that these, especially the former, were within reach of scholarly men and men of affairs at the time when the Pennsylvania instrument was framed; and other reasons will manifest themselves as we proceed with this study.

Censors were appointed at Rome after 443 B.C.[1] They were usually (after the Second Punic War) those who had been consuls. They held office for five years, but their active work was done during the first eighteen months of the period for which they were elected. They exercised supervision over certain Roman customs. They could expel a senator, deprive a knight of his horse, regulate the public taxes, inspect the public buildings, and divide the people into their proper centuries and classes. The position of a censor was one of the most honorable and powerful in the Roman republic, and it existed for four centuries, or until, under the empire, the control of that office was assumed by the state.

This institution of censors bore a certain resemblance to an institution connected with the Spartan state, known as the ephors. This office was important from early times, and it furnished a check on the active government, representing as it did the community of Sparta. The ephors were five in number, and they held office for one year. It was their duty to superintend public morals and education. They exercised a strong influence on legislation and even checked the action of the executive.[2]

[1] Kennett's "Roman Antiquities," London, 1769, fourteenth edition, pp. 112–114. Kennett's book is quoted as one of those most likely to have been examined by "the fathers."
[2] Bojeson's "Greek and Roman Antiquities," pp. 58, 59.

Plato evidently has a similar institution in view when he asserts, in his "Laws,"[1] that guardians should be sought who are incorruptible, "to establish more firmly institutions in the state which are good already, and amend what is deficient." He would have the nocturnal council, composed of men trained by travel and experience, meet daily to consider matters of public importance; and he would regard this as "a guard set according to law for the salvation of the state."

Montesquieu, in his "Spirit of the Laws," draws on the Roman plan of public censors and the Greek ephorate as very useful methods for keeping public officials and laws subservient to the people.[2] He recites that the Spartan, conscious of this check, feared the tribunal of public opinion far more than did the Athenian official, who well knew the weakness of his state in passing censure on his public acts.

About 1762 Rousseau's "Contrat Social" appeared, which devoted a chapter to his proposed method by which the sovereign people could hold their magistrates in check. He felt that modern nations had lost that power which was once so salutary,—"chez les Romains et mieux chez les Lacédémoniens."[3] His theory was, ". . . that the censor may be useful in preserving the customs, but never in reestablishing them. Establish censors while the laws are vigorous; as soon as they become weakened everything is past hope; nothing legitimate has force when the laws have none. The censor maintains the standard of morals by preventing the corruption of opinions, by preserving their rectitude through wise applications, sometimes even by fixing them when they are uncertain."

It is evident that Rousseau, having in mind the censors of Rome and the Greek ephors, planned an institution resembling that which we are studying.

The American colonists of the third quarter of the eighteenth century were men who had had occasion to study the nature and limitations of popular government. There were

[1] Plato's "Dialogues" (Jowett's trans.), Vol. V. Sects. 951, 961, 968.
[2] Montesquieu, "Works" (trans., 1777), Vol. I., Chap. VII., pp. 61–63.
[3] Rousseau, "Œuvres Complètes," Paris, 1793, T. II. pp. 210–213.

educated men among them, men who had been liberally instructed in American colleges, whose courses of study were principally in the classics. No classical student could fail to know something of the history of Greece and Rome; while to men like the Adamses, Franklin, Dickinson, and many whose names are less widely known, Greek and Roman history would furnish foundation studies in popular government. There were ample sources in English for studies of classic models of government. In 1769 Kennett's "Roman Antiquities" had passed to its fourteenth edition, and was probably accessible to the students in every American college, while similar studies in the antiquities of Greece, one may reasonably infer, would have been equally accessible. Controversial letters in the newspapers abounded with signatures drawn from Greek and Roman classics. "Spartanus," "Cato," and "Cassandra" honored the names of pamphleteers not only in Philadelphian but in other American papers; and many a statesman of antiquity was represented as the responsible person for dissertations on the relation of the people to legitimate government.

It would be presuming contrary to reasonable inference to assume that these men were not acquainted with the views of Montesquieu and Rousseau on popular government. The works of the former had been before the students of statecraft in Europe for a quarter of a century, while Rousseau's "Contrat Social" began its radical mission ten years later.

Rousseau was the apostle of extreme democracy. The leaven of his influence was manifest in Europe during the last quarter of the eighteenth century; and so it came about that the Council of Censors has a European history, which we proceed first to recount.

At the height of the French Revolution Robespierre, on May 10, 1793, delivered a speech in the National Convention, wherein he says, in the course of a great debate[1] on the proposed Constitution of France, that the executive power

[1] *Le Moniteur*, Lundi, 13 Mai, 1793, p. 584, second column.

is limited by the *Corps Législatif,* and that every public functionary should be amenable for his conduct to a tribunal of the people; that a representative government fails of its legitimate ends that does not obey and cannot be compelled to obey the mandate of the popular will.

We quote these words: "Il est naturel que le corps chargé de faire les lois, surveille ceux qui sont commis pour les faire exécuter. Les membres de l'agence exécutive seront donc tenus de rendre compte de leur gestion au corps législatif. En cas de prévarication, il ne pourra pas les punir, parce qu'il ne faut pas lui laisser ce moyen de s'emparer de la puissance exécutive; mais il les accusera devant un tribunal populaire dont l'unique fonction sera de connaître des prévarications des fonctionnaires publics."[1]

May 13, 1793, the National Convention adopted a programme by which its deliberations on the new constitution should be governed. The twelfth item in that programme read as follows:

"Chapitre XII. Comment le peuple exerce lui-même sa souveraineté sur les fonctionnaires publics et sur les actes."[2]

On the 10th of June, 1793, Hérault de Séchelles, representing the Committee of Public Safety, delivered a speech in defence of the project of a constitution which he had brought forward, and in which he recognized the Council of Censors as an essential feature to make the government of France not alone republican, but democratic. Chapter XV. of the proposed French Constitution of 1793 read as follows:

"Du grand juré national, Article Premier:

I. "Le grand juré est institué pour garantir les citoyens de l'oppression du corps législatif et du conseil. Tout citoyen opprimé par un acte particulier, a droit d'y recourir.

II. "La liste des jurés est composée d'un citoyen, élu dans chaque département par les assemblées primaires. Le

---

[1] *Le Moniteur*, Lundi, 13 Mai, 1793, p. 584, second column.
[2] Ibid., Lundi, 20 Mai, 1793, p. 608, first column.

grand juré est renouvelé tous les ans avec le corps législatif.

III. "Il n'applique point les peines. Il renvoie devant les tribunaux.

IV. "Les noms des jurés sont déposés dans une urne au sein du corps législatif." [1]

In defence of this so-called "national grand jury," or Council of Censors, Hérault used these words: "Nous en avons cherché le remède dans la formation d'un grand juré, destiné à venger le citoyen opprimé dans sa personne, des vexations (s'il pouvait en survenir)—du corps législatif et du conseil: tribunal imposant et consolateur, créé par le peuple, à la même heure, et dans les mêmes formes qu'il créé ses représentans; auguste asyle de la liberté, où nulle vexation ne serait pardonnée, et où le mandataire coupable n'échapperait pas plus à la justice qu'à l'opinion." [2]

Hérault de Séchelles's "Rapport" [3] is full of enthusiasm for the Council of Censors. He advocates its adoption and defends its good features with more emphasis than one finds in Rousseau's chapter on "The Censors" in his "Contrat Social."

In the French Constitution as adopted in 1795 this provision was omitted. The excesses of the French democracy following the Convention of 1793 caused those in authority to be unwilling to place so much power in the hands of the people as the plan of Hérault de Séchelles contemplated. The next attempt in Europe to make use of this instrument of popular government occurred when Maria Pagano drew up a constitution for the Neapolitan republic in 1799. [4] This was modelled on the French Constitution of 1793. For the directory it substituted a system of archons, who could hold office only two years. In matters of appeal, one

---

[1] *Le Moniteur*, 19 Juin, 1793, p. 732, second and third columns.

[2] Ibid., Jeudi, 13 Juin, 1793, p. 707, second column.

[3] Kindly lent by the library of Cornell University.

[4] "Biographie Universelle," Paris, 1844, T. LXXVI., LXXVII. Among his works is mentioned "VII. Projet de constitution pour a république Napolitaine, 1799."

section of one tribunal might appeal to another section; or one section of one department could appeal to another department. This was especially accomplished by an ephorate and by a tribunal of censure, which was a distinguishing feature of the Neapolitan constitution. The ephorate was a sort of conservative senate, and its duty was to keep the desires of the different branches within reasonable limits and to place a check on usurpations. The tribunal of censure was an imitation of the domestic censure which, according to Montesquieu, assisted in a remarkable manner in the preservation of the customs of the ancient republic of Rome.

This constitution, like that of 1793 in France, was never tested by use. French reverses in the north of Italy had their consequences in Naples. Pagano gave up the pen for the sword, and with other members of his provisional government fell into the hands of the enemy. He perished on the scaffold October 6, 1800.

At the close of the eighteenth century, in Europe, the method of regulating governments by a tribunal created and controlled by the people had no abiding place on the Continent. Montesquieu and Rousseau had drawn on the Greek ephors and the Roman censors for a popular plan for regulating government officials; but it was only a theory, and the excesses of the French Revolution prevented its having a fair trial in practice.

III. PRELIMINARIES IN AMERICA.

In America the political doctrines of Rousseau took root and bore fruit; but they were modified by the more conservative views of Locke. Traces of Rousseau's views may perhaps be seen in the opening paragraphs of Paine's " Common Sense ;" and Paine's connection with the Pennsylvania radicals who made the constitution of 1776 is well known. There had long been a feeling of unrest in the colonies, a feeling that the people should control their political affairs; that the governed should of right command their servants or governors. It was in the air. There were conservatives who sought only to modify the policy of the crown in certain details. They had no desire to break up the foundations of the government and build on a new foundation. The radical party would break with the mother country; it would go back to first principles; it would stand by the rights of man. Of the former party John Dickinson was a type; of the latter were Paine, Franklin, and Jefferson. In 1776 the radical party had succeeded in securing the independence of the colonies.

Before passing to consider at length the relation of the Council of Censors to the constitutions of Pennsylvania and Vermont, a slight digression may throw a side-light on the views which prevailed with reference to popular government in the country at large.

In 1776 a pamphlet was published with the title, " The People the Best Governors." [1] It took the ground that sovereignty lies with the people; that the Legislature has no right to appoint agents to restrain governmental action, because this appointing power lies with the people in virtue of sovereignty, and sovereignty cannot be delegated. It suggested a senate or council, to be elected by the people, to check legislation, resembling what is now known as a State Senate, but with a partial resemblance also to a Council of Censors. The foregoing statement of the need of popular checks on representative government is followed by a statement of the specific method to be employed:

" 4thly, That the people chuse annually by ballot in their town meetings, a council, consisting of twelve persons, through the government at large, whose business shall be to help in preparing matters for the consideration of the assembly, to assist them with their advice. And, lastly, it shall be their duty to inquire into every essential defect in the regulations of government, and to give the people seasonable notice in a public way, with their opinion respecting the matter."

The view of the pamphleteer seems to have been that the people are the best, the real governors, and that a limited number of men, duly elected, may constitute a regulative

---

[1] Text in Chase's " History of Dartmouth College," Appendix D.

board. The Rousseau idea is evidently involved in the suggestion, even though the Latin name of " Censors" is absent, and a permanent upper House is contemplated.

Only two American States have employed the Council of Censors in their fundamental law,—Pennsylvania from 1776 to 1790, and Vermont from 1777 to 1869—almost a century. To these two examples most of the further consideration of this subject will be devoted.

In the constitution which Rev. Samuel Houston drew up for the State of Frankland in 1785 there was a provision for a Council of Safety to be elected once in five years. Its general features were quite like those of the Council of Censors. This constitution failed of ratification, and when a constitution was made later for Tennessee this radical feature did not appear.[1]

IV. PENNSYLVANIA: THE CONSTITUTION OF 1776.

On May 15, 1776, the Continental Congress voted that the colonies be requested " to adopt such government as shall in the opinion of the representatives of the people best conduce to the happiness and safety of their constituents in particular and Americans in general." [2] Acting on this request, the citizens of Pennsylvania elected delegates to a Constitutional Convention which met July 5, 1776, and continued its sittings to September 28 of the same year.

The framing of a new constitution for the province of Pennsylvania involved many interests. It lined up the two parties, or political interests, of Pennsylvania on the same principles that had divided them ten years earlier. Those who opposed the continuance of the proprietary government in 1764 favored the plan for a new constitution, favored the extension of the suffrage, favored severing the

---

[1] Ramsay's "History of Tennessee," pp. 282 *et passim; American Historical Magazine,* 1896. The New York Tammany Society, as is shown by its manuscript records, had in its early days officials called censors.

[2] "Journals of Congress," Vol. II. p. 166.

tics which had existed between the colony and Great Britain.
In this party were the radicals of Philadelphia and of the
more thickly populated sections of the adjacent counties,
and with them consorted the Scotch-Irish and Presbyterians,
and the inhabitants of the remoter sections, who felt that
they had grievances against the proprietary government.
The Quaker and German elements were conservative. They
had stood for the retention of the proprietary government;
they stood for good order, for keeping political power in the
hands of those who were known to be safe. They dis-
trusted the people whom a fifty-pound requirement in
property disfranchised. Opposed to the unjust efforts for
taxation on the part of the crown in 1764, they now opposed independence and rendered only a lukewarm assist-
ance to those who were struggling against Great Britain.

On June 18, 1776, a Provincial Conference, with Thomas
McKean as president, assembled at Carpenters' Hall in
Philadelphia and continued its sittings until June 25, when
it adjourned. This conference consisted of ninety-seven
delegates representing the people of the various counties
of the province.[1] They decided that in considering all
questions each county should have one vote; that they approved the resolution of Congress calling for a new constitution for Pennsylvania; that "every associator" in the
province should be entitled to vote for members of the
convention, provided he were twenty-one years of age and
had resided one year in the province; provided also that he
had paid taxes, and should take oath that he did not owe
allegiance to Great Britain. They recommended that the
proposed convention should consist of eight delegates from
each county, Philadelphia City and County being counted
separately, that each member of the convention should
be a qualified voter, and that he should be required to
renounce allegiance to the crown and assert belief in
the Holy Trinity and the inspiration of the Scriptures.
After issuing an appeal to the people of the province, and

[1] "Proceedings and Minutes," pp. 35–45.

setting July 8 as the day for the new election, the conference adjourned.

Such was the authority for calling the convention. It represented the will of the people expressed in a way for which the proprietary government of Pennsylvania had not provided, but one as legitimate as that by which the Declaration of Independence had been adopted.

Constitution-making was new work for the American colonists, and they felt their way slowly. But the air was full of suggestions. It was proposed that the Assembly choose from its number twenty members to be a legislative council, this being preferable to a council chosen by the people; that no alteration should be made in the " Charter" " without the consent of two-thirds of the people testified by voting by ballot." It was further suggested[1] that the members form a plan of government, submit it to the people by printing it in the newspapers, and then adjourn; that the people should choose a new convention which should have power to make alterations in the new constitution or confirm it. Another writer appeals to the people on the necessity of framing a new constitution, cites the governments of Greece and Rome as examples, says that this province is worse off than the other colonies in that the " House of Assembly is a part of that power from which we are trying to break away," and that it is disqualified for business. Daniel Roberdeau added the protests, for similar reasons, of the " inhabitants of the city and liberties of Philadelphia."[2] In Philadelphia and adjacent counties, however, a remonstrance against a new government was framed, and signed by six thousand names.[3] " A Freeman" in a later paper[4] asserts that the remonstrance does not represent the people of the province, and that the protesters have no desire to disturb the power of the Assembly, but

[1] *Pennsylvania Evening Post*, No. 232, July 16, 1776.
[2] Ibid., No. 208, May 21, 1776.
[3] Ibid., No. 216, June 8, 1776.
[4] Ibid., No. 217, June 11, 1776.

to frame a constitution, a work which the Assembly could not do.

Suggestions were made not only as to framing a plan of government, but as to keeping it in order. There seemed to be a desire to adopt a plan whereby the people should not only make a constitution, but to them should be confided[1] the power to alter and amend the same. John Adams's suggestion[2] was that the Legislature devise the methods of electing representatives " as in Connecticut," or that it might enlarge the period for which they should be chosen " to seven years, or three years, or for life, or may make any other alterations which the society shall find productive of its ease, its safety, its freedom, or in one word its happiness."

Another writer under the *nom de guerre* of Demophilus may perhaps be fairly regarded as having made the direct preliminary suggestion for the Council of Censors. He wrote as follows :[3]

" Probably a decennial meeting of delegates to examine the state of the constitution and conduct of the government would not be an imprudent provision for keeping the constitution in health and vigor, by having an opportunity to see that it did not depart from its first principles. This would be effectually holding the supreme power in its *only* safe repository, the *hands of the people.*"

The election of delegates took place July 8. The conservatives took little or no part in this election, and the result was that the party in favor of a more democratic government were in a large majority.[4]

On July 16 the delegates met, organized, and made the

[1] *Pennsylvania Evening Post*, No. 217, June 11, 1776.

[2] "Thoughts on Government, Applicable to the Present State of the American Colonies, Philadelphia, 1776: Printed by John Dunlap." John Adams's " Works," Vol. IV. p. 197.

[3] "The Genuine Principles of the Ancient Saxon and English Constitution, Philadelphia: Printed and sold by Robert Bell, in Third Street, MDCCLXXVI.," p. 38.

[4] Marshall's "Diary," p. 83. Attention is called to this passage by Mr. P. L. Ford in the "Political Science Quarterly," Vol. X., 1895.

required profession of political faith,[1] renouncing all allegiance to the British crown, declaring faith in the Holy Trinity, and pledging themselves " to establish and support a government in this province on the authority of the people only."[2]   Benjamin Franklin was elected president, and after electing the other necessary officers and clerks the convention was ready for business.

On July 18 a committee was appointed to bring in " an essay" for a frame of government; an addition to it was made July 25, when it stood as follows: Owen Biddle, Colonel Bull, Reverend William Van Horne, John Jacobs, Colonel Ross, Colonel James Smith, Jonathan Hoge, Jacob Morgan, Colonel Stroud, Colonel Thomas Smith, Robert Martin, Colonel Timothy Matlack, James Cannon, Colonel Potter, David Rittenhouse, Robert Whitehill, and Bertram Galbreath.[3]   On July 25 the convention endorsed the Declaration of Independence and pledged themselves to " support and maintain the freedom and independence of this and the other United States of America at the utmost risk of " their lives and fortunes.[4]

On September 28 the frame of government was confirmed and ratified by the convention in a declaration in which were these words :[5]

"We the representatives of the freemen of Pennsylvania, in general convention met for the express purpose of framing such a government . . . do, by virtue of the authority vested in us by our constituents, ordain, declare and establish the following declaration of rights and frame of government, to be the constitution of this commonwealth and to remain in force therein forever unaltered, except in such articles as shall hereafter, on experience, be found to require improvements, and which shall by the same authority of the people, fairly delegated, as this frame of government directs, be amended or improved for the more effectual obtaining and securing the great end and design of all government herein before mentioned."

The constitution contained several curious provisions. It provided for a unicameral Legislature, and vested the

---

[1] "Proceedings and Minutes," p. 46.
[2] Ibid., p. 39.   [3] Ibid., pp. 48, 49.   [4] Ibid., p. 49.   [5] Ibid., p. 55.

executive power in a president and council. It provided for amending the constitution and keeping the government under the control of the people by a Council of Censors. To this council was committed the initiative in setting on foot reforms in the fundamental law and certain inquisitorial powers as to the manner in which public officials did their duties. The council was also to see that taxes and general expenditures were justly levied and discharged. The provisions respecting it were those which have been quoted on the first page of this article (Section 47 of the constitution).

Who drew up this frame of government, and to whom are we indebted for Section 47 of the constitution, the clause treating of the Council of Censors? The minutes and proceedings of the convention throw little light on this question, since they do not contain the debates nor a full record of the proceedings.

The committee for bringing in a frame of government contained some eminent men, men of high repute; but it is probable that these had less to do with the actual work of making the frame of government than some who were less widely and favorably known, belonging to the extremely radical wing of the popular party.

It is reasonably certain that David Rittenhouse had little or no part in it,[1] and the same authority attributes but little of the work to Benjamin Franklin, although Timothy Matlack assured Richard Bache that his " venerable father-in-law was one" to whom the " Convention paid the highest respect" in providing for a Legislature of a single branch.[2]

The Council of Censors is attributed to James Cannon and George Bryan;[3] George Bryan was not a member of the convention, however; hence the fact that he is charged with its authorship in connection with James Cannon shows

[1] Barton's " Life of David Rittenhouse," p. 336, note.
[2] *Pennsylvania Gazette*, March 31, 1779. " A Candid Examination of the Report of the Minority," pp. 51, 52.
[3] Graydon's " Memoirs," pp. 285-288.

the influences that worked together for providing this radical feature of the Pennsylvania constitution. As each of these men is charged with being the author[1] of the constitution, one may reasonably infer that it grew out of the combined views of the radical wing of the people's party, in which were Timothy Matlack, James Cannon, George Bryan, Dr. Thomas Young, and Thomas Paine.[2] Two, Matlack and Cannon, were members of the convention and of the committee for drawing up a frame of government; and the fact that George Bryan, an outsider, is associated with it leads one to infer that the views of the entire group found expression, in a measure, in the frame of government.

James Cannon was a Scotchman, came to Philadelphia in 1765, was a tutor, and later a professor of mathematics, in the College of Philadelphia, was active in the " Associates of Philadelphia," author of the " Cassandra" letters, and secretary of the " American Manufactory." He died in 1782.[3] One contemporary writer calls him " a fanatical school-master," and another distinguishes him thus : " Of his colleague, Mr. Cannon, it may not be uncharitable to presume, that having little knowledge of men, and that scholastic predilection for the antique in liberty, which

[1] "Remarks on the Powers of the Council of Censors in Pennsylvania," Philadelphia, 1784, pp. 13, a pamphlet in the library of the Historical Society of Pennsylvania. " It was composed in a hurry, I am told, by a fanatical school-master while the wisest and best men in the state were in the field."

[2] Marshall's " Remembrancer," p. 71, March 15, 1776, " Past five went to James Cannon's. Drank coffee with Timothy Matlack ;" p. 83, May 25, " Thence to James Cannon's who was gone out with Timothy Matlack to meet sundry county members at Norrington ;" ibid., May 30, " Dr. Young came there [Cannon's] to see me ;" p. 84, May 31, " Went from there to James Cannon's, found a select company of friends of the liberties of America ;" p. 91, July 3, " Near nine [P.M.] went to meet the Committee of Privates with others at Thorne's School Room where three speakers ; viz., James Cannon, Timothy Matlack [and] Dr. Young flourished on the necessity of choosing eight persons to be proposed to the people for our Representatives in Convention."

[3] PENNA. MAG., Vol. III. p. 198. Graydon's "Memoirs," pp. 285–287.

generally falls to the lot of a pedagogue, he acted accordingly."[1] This certainly gives color to the view that Mr. Cannon may have had in mind the Council of Ephors of the Greeks and the censors of the Roman constitution. But the coterie to which he belonged may have been familiar with Rousseau's views and he may have taken the idea from "The Social Contract."[2]

George Bryan was an Irishman,[3] a great reader, fluent talker, intensely opposed "to whatever was English," and an ardent democrat. His interests were with the popular party, for with them lay his only chances for a public career, since by birth, training, and the lack of property he was unacceptable to the conservative party. Seven years later, when elected a member of the Council of Censors, he was attacked and derided in the public prints of Philadelphia, called "Censor-General of Pennsylvania," and "*spem gregis.*"[4] "Z" in an open letter to a newspaper exclaims, "Judge Bryan for the city of Philadelphia! *Hinc illæ lachrymæ.*" He is charged with being poor, with being actuated by the sentiments of neither morals nor religion, and with violating the very laws he has taken oath to support.[5]

Timothy Matlack was a Quaker and a native of New Jersey. He was a member of the Provincial Conference of June 18, 1776, and of the Constitutional Convention; secretary of state most of the time till March 25, 1783, and member of the Council of Safety from July, 1776, to March, 1777. He was a fighting Quaker, and was disowned by the Society for the part he took in the Revolution.[6]

Dr. Young had lived in Boston and in Albany, was ap-

[1] "Remarks on the Powers of the Council of Censors" (Philadelphia, 1784), p. 13; *Pennsylvania Gazette*, No. 2802, February 25, 1784; Marshall's "Diary" and "Remembrancer."

[2] Loc. cit.

[3] Graydon's "Memoirs," pp. 287, 288.

[4] *Pennsylvania Gazette*, No. 2829, August 25, 1784.

[5] Ibid., No. 2782, October 8, 1783.

[6] PENNA. MAG., Vol. IV. p. 92, Vol. XVI. p. 315.
**

pointed a surgeon in the army, and the following year, 1776, urged Vermont to adopt the Pennsylvania constitution. Of Thomas Paine, whose letters, subscribed "Common Sense," appeared frequently in the Pennsylvania papers, it seems unnecessary to speak.

The framers of the constitution evidently intended to build principally upon new lines and avoid all features of the proprietary government that had proved objectionable.[1] They retained the unicameral Legislature and annual elections, but provided for manhood suffrage based on the payment of taxes and one year's residence.[2] The executive power was vested not in a single person, but in a president and Executive Council; all bills were to be printed before they passed to a third reading, for the consideration of the people, and then they were to go to the next session of the Legislature for passage. Naturalization was made easy, one year's residence being required for the privilege of voting and two for holding office.

The provision for amending the constitution early gave rise to criticism. Benjamin Rush in a letter to General Wayne (September 24, 1776) expressed the feeling that the constitution had many weaknesses, and complained that the governor and council had no veto power, but hoped the Council of Censors would remedy this in seven years.[3] Even one year later Joseph Reed in a letter to the General Council of Pennsylvania lamented "that the constitution has not provided a more adequate and earlier mode of improving what is right, and amending what is wrong."[4] He regarded this as a weakness, thought seven years too long to wait for needed changes, and that the result would be either "spiritless languor" or "convulsion."

On September 28 the convention completed its labors

---

[1] Letter of Thomas Smith to Arthur St. Clair, "St. Clair Papers," Vol. I. p. 222.

[2] "Proceedings and Minutes," pp. 54–66; "St. Clair Papers," Vol. I. p. 272.

[3] Stillé's "Major-General Wayne and the Pennsylvania Line," p. 40.

[4] "Life and Correspondence of Joseph Reed," Vol. I. p. 302.

and disbanded.[1] The constitution was not ratified by the people. Fears were entertained of Howe's invasion, and hence it was next to impossible to place the instrument in proper form before the people for their consideration.

V. Pennsylvania: The Inauguration of the Constitution.

On October 17 a caucus was held[2] for the purpose of " devising methods for setting aside sundry improper and unconstitutional rules laid down by the late convention in what they call their Plan or Frame of Government." After some deliberation, and agreeing to suggest some changes and present them in print for the consideration of the people of the State, it was decided to hold a general meeting in the State-House yard the following Monday afternoon, October 21. About fifteen hundred persons were present, Colonel Bayard presiding. The speakers opposed to the late convention were Colonel McKean and John Dickinson; in its favor, James Cannon, Timothy Matlack, Dr. Young, and Colonel Smith, of York County.[3] An adjournment was taken at night to the following day. At this adjourned meeting the resolves for changing the new government were carried by a large majority.

The result of this meeting was the formulation of twenty-nine specific objections to the frame of government. " It is the sense of this meeting that the people are generally and greatly dissatisfied with the said constitution." Four specific resolutions were made with reference to the matter of amending the constitution. In effect they were that the amending of the constitution was committed to a Council of Censors, and that it required a two-thirds vote of that body to effect a change in the constitution; that seven years must elapse before such amendments could be made, and that this was a violation of the rights of the freemen of the State; that it is the sense of the meeting that the people are greatly

---

[1] " Proceedings and Minutes."
[2] Marshall's " Diary," p. 97.   [3] Ibid.

dissatisfied with the constitution; that the Assembly ought
to have full power to make needed changes in the constitution; and that these changes should be submitted to the
people for their consideration before they are finally passed
upon.[1]

Efforts were made to reach the people of the different
counties[2] to secure their concurrence in the proceedings
which resulted in the condemnation of so many features of
the constitution. At the election the conservatives took
little or no part, and the friends of the constitution thereby
had a majority.[3] But when the Legislature assembled (November 28) it was found that the minority opposed to the
constitution was large enough to prevent the transaction of
business; and matters were at a stand-still when Congress,
fearing the appearance of the British in Pennsylvania,
threatened to assume the reins of government for Pennsylvania if the Assembly did not proceed with business.

At this point John Dickinson, member from Philadelphia,
proposed to assist in organizing the government and doing
business, provided that the Assembly would agree to a
measure seeking to call a convention to revise the objectionable features of the constitution. His proposition was not
accepted and he resigned.[4] The Assembly adjourned December 14 and did not come together until January 13; but
no business could be done. The new government was not
organized until March 4, when Thomas Wharton, Jr., was
elected president and George Bryan vice-president of the
Supreme Executive Council. The inauguration ceremonies
took place March 5, and then the government of Pennsylvania under the new constitution was ready for business.[5]

Mr. Wharton, the president of the Supreme Executive
Council, felt that the constitution was not all that it should

---

[1] *Pennsylvania Evening Post*, No. 274, October 22, 1776.
[2] Marshall's "Diary," p. 99.
[3] Stillé's "John Dickinson," Vol. I. p. 208; Marshall's "Diary," p. 103.
[4] "Thomas Wharton, Jr.," by Anne H. Wharton, PENNA. MAG.,
Vol. V.
[5] PENNA. MAG., Vol. V. pp. 437–439.

be; but he thought it wiser to proceed with it, and do the best he could, rather than leave Pennsylvania with no government when she was so hard pressed by an enemy in an adjoining State and by dissension among her own people.[1]

VI. PENNSYLVANIA: THE NEW CONSTITUTION AND 'ITS ADMINISTRATION, 1776–1783.

The constitution of Pennsylvania was launched upon a stormy sea. Howe and his army threatened to invade the State, and the political dissension added to the confusion. The political factions seemed to subdivide on religious lines.[2] The Whigs divided: some wanted to revise the constitution, while others wanted it kept as it was framed.[3] The laws were disregarded. The trouble "brought the dregs to the top."

The influence of Cannon, Matlack, and Dr. Young was still felt. In the opinion of their opponents, they held "back the strength of the State by urging the execution of their rascally Government in preference to supporting measures for repelling the common enemy."[4]

The two chief points of attack in the constitution were the Legislature, with its single House, and the method of amending. The new Legislature was called a "mob government;" it was believed to appeal to the passions and interests of its supporters.[5] Joseph Reed, president of the Supreme Executive Council in 1778, felt that the method of amending was a weakness of the constitution, and particularly because of the seven-year time limit.[6]

Richard Bache, Benjamin Franklin's son-in-law, pre-

---

[1] He was elected councillor by only fourteen votes out of six thousand voters. "Remarks on Powers of Council of Censors," *Pennsylvania Gazette*, No. 2802, February 25, 1784.

[2] James Allen's "Diary," February 17, 1777; PENNA. MAG., Vol. IX. p. 279.

[3] Ibid., June 6, 1777; PENNA. MAG., Vol. IX. pp. 282, 283.

[4] Stillé's "Wayne," p. 68; letter of Dr. B. Rush to General Wayne.

[5] Ibid., p. 69.

[6] "Life and Correspondence of Joseph Reed," Vol. I. p. 302.

sented two petitions for having the constitution amended.
The first he offered in June, 1777, in his capacity of chairman of the Board of War,[1] and the second was addressed
to the citizens of Pennsylvania, and purported to come from
the members of the Republican Society, Richard Bache,
chairman. Among the eighty-five signatures were those
of George Clymer, Benjamin Rush, Robert Morris, and
Ephraim Blaine. Their petition specified, as among the objectionable features, the single Legislature and the Council
of Censors, suggested a second legislative House, denied
that it was a " House of Lords," because it would be elected
by the people, and set forth that a Legislature of two Houses
would not be composed of two orders of men, as the Roman
government was. Their views of the censors may be best
expressed by quoting their language :

" What shall we say of the Council of Censors? Here indeed is a
novelty of the most dangerous and alarming kind.

" Our constitution-makers, not satisfied with the habitual despotism
of a single and uncontrouled Legislature, have appointed stated seasons
for extraordinary efforts of lawless power.

" They have instituted a jubilee of tyranny to be celebrated at the end
of every seven years. Glorious period! When the foundations of government shall be torn up! When anarchy and licentiousness and force
shall roam unawed and unrestrained! When there shall be no fixed laws
to which you can appeal for the justification of your conduct! When
there shall be no courts to which you can have recourse for protection!
When trials by jury, those odious obstructions that lie in the way of
tyrants, shall be happily removed!

" Are you pleased with the prospect? If you wish not to feel it real-
ized by direful experience, lay hold eagerly upon the present opportunity
which is offered you of preventing it, by voting for a new constitution
to abolish this part of the constitution."[2]

The Legislature so far yielded to the demands of the
petitioners that, on June 17, 1777, it voted to ascertain the
wishes of the people as to calling a new convention.[3] This
measure failed, however, in consequence of Howe's invasion.

[1] " Pennsylvania Archives," Vol. I. p. 54.
[2] *Pennsylvania Gazette*, No. 2545, March 24, 1779.
[3] " Proceedings and Minutes," p. 111.

On November 28, 1778, a resolution passed the Legislature which gave the people an opportunity of voting, on March 25 of the following year, for or against a convention; and it specified the points which would come before such a convention, among them the abolition of the Council of Censors.[1] Following this movement came petitions in opposition from thirteen thousand inhabitants, and February 27, 1779, the resolution of November 28, 1778, was rescinded by a vote of forty-seven to seven.

From this time to the meeting of the Council of Censors in 1783 nothing outside of newspaper criticism was done in the direction of changing the constitution of Pennsylvania.[2]

VII. PENNSYLVANIA: THE COUNCIL OF CENSORS AND ITS WORK.

On November 13, 1783, the Council of Censors provided for in Section 47 of the constitution met in Philadelphia, and organized with Frederick A. Muhlenberg as president.[3] On November 19 a committee, consisting of Fitzsimmons, Smiley, Irvine, and Reed, was appointed to consider and report as to whether the constitution had been kept inviolate in every part. On Thursday, December 4, the council resolved that on Monday, the 15th, it would, in committee of the whole, consider whether there were any need of amending any article of the constitution.[4] On December 17 it was ordered that the committee appointed to see whether the constitution had been kept inviolate should inquire as to whether the executive and legislative branches of the government had gone beyond the powers assigned to them under the constitution. On January 1, 1784, the council, in committee of the whole, Richard Mc-Allister in the chair, considered the defects of the constitution and as to whether amendments were needed. On January 2 the report of the committee of the whole was

---

[1] "Proceedings and Minutes," p. 111.

[2] Ibid., p. 112; "Life and Correspondence of Joseph Reed," Vol. I. pp. 46, 47.

[3] Ibid., p. 67.   [4] Ibid.

read to the House, and it was resolved that some articles of the constitution were defective and absolutely needed alteration and amendment. At this time a committee, consisting of Miles, Fitzsimmons, St. Clair, Hartley, and Arndt, was appointed to report on the defective articles of the constitution. On January 3 the committee was instructed to report the alterations and amendments that were needed in the constitution.

Two committees reported in part on January 17, and their reports were ordered to lie on the table,—the committee appointed to consider whether the constitution had been preserved inviolate and the committee appointed to propose needed amendments.[1] On January 19 the council considered the report of the committee on the defects and alterations of the constitution. This report " was read a second time by paragraphs, considered, amended, and adopted."

Among the defects suggested were these : the Legislature with one House, the executive power vested in a president and council, the dependence of the judiciary upon the Legislature, frequent rotation in office, and unequal representation. Among the changes or amendments proposed were these : that the Legislature consist of a House of Representatives and a legislative council ; that the executive power be vested in a governor, who should have a veto power ; that the Assembly should be limited to one hundred members and the legislative council to twenty-nine members ; that judges should be appointed by the governor to serve during good behavior, with fixed salaries, and that Section 47, dealing with the Council of Censors, should be omitted. Each amendment proposed by the committee was passed by the council by a vote of twelve favoring and nine opposing.

At this point a controversy arose on the construction to be placed on the report of the committee on amendments.[2] The minority stoutly maintained that it involved the idea of calling a convention to consider the amendments pro-

[1] " Proceedings and Minutes."   [2] Ibid., pp. 77–82.

posed; and that, having failed to obtain a two-thirds vote of the Council of Censors, no appeal could be made to the people to elect delegates to a Constitutional Convention.

In their dissentient report they maintained that no appeal could be made to the people without violating Section 47 of the constitution, reciting the history of the action of the committee on amendments from its appointment on January 2 to the adoption of its report on January 19; that changes should not be lightly made; that at the end of every seven years such changes could be made, and that this council had now decided that no change at present is necessary; that if Section 47 is now violated, other dangerous innovations may be made; that the present constitution was made in great harmony; that it had been the means of carrying the State through great crises, and if it should be changed now the responsibility must rest with the majority; that the constitution had well stood the test of trial; that the proposed changes would make the government expensive; that if Section 47 were abolished, no method of changing the constitution, except revolution, would be left to the people.

On January 21, by a vote of thirteen to nine, the council resolved, " That the council did not then nor at any time since acquiesce or agree in the opinion that the vote of January 2 determined the question as to calling a convention." [1] The majority at this point framed and adopted an appeal to the citizens of Pennsylvania, and adjourned to meet June 5.

The appeal of the majority set forth that the greatest question before the council was the constitution itself; that it was faulty as compared with the constitutions of other States; that a majority of this council, but not two-thirds, desire to change certain parts of it as dangerous to the liberties of the people; that no reasonable motive for the opposition to these measures can be assigned; that the constitution was framed in the heat of party passions, when a foreign foe menaced the State, and when many of the citizens were absent on military service; that many citizens

[1] " Proceedings and Minutes," p. 80.

opposed to it at the outset submitted to it only on the understanding that it should be amended; that seven years had elapsed and a minority that does not represent one-third of the people binds the majority, as if afraid to trust the people to frame a government for themselves; that the sovereign people of the State could decide whether the present constitution was agreeable to them; that the changes proposed were not experiments, but had been well tried in sister States; that as the amending of the constitution was the most important matter for the council to consider, and as the minority were not likely to yield, an adjournment should be taken to June 1.

This was followed by the appeal of the minority to the people of the State, setting forth that the majority of the Council of Censors had appointed a committee of their own to prepare and bring in a new frame of government; that time had been wasted and needless expense involved by the obstinacy of the small majority in trying to have a new constitution made instead of considering the infractions of the old one; that the single executive or governor would be dangerous; that the minority was manfully struggling to preserve the present constitution; that the proposed second branch of the Legislature was in effect a House of Lords, and that the governor's powers should not be extended as proposed.[1]

On February 11 followed " A Candid Examination of the Address of the Minority by One of the Majority," wherein it was declared that because ten thought one way and twelve thought another way, and a two-thirds vote is necessary for calling a convention, therefore the minority felt that the question of calling a convention could not longer be an object of deliberation,—the question of calling a convention never really came before the council; it was agreed generally that the constitution was defective, and the committee was appointed to suggest alterations and changes that were needed; it was denied that time had been wasted; much

[1] *Pennsylvania Gazette*, No 2798, January 28, 1784, "Address of the Minority of the Council of Censors to the Citizens of Pennsylvania."

laborious work had been done, and in regard to adjournment, the majority wished to make the time to March 1, but as people in the back counties wanted to be at home in planting time, the limit was set for June 1; as to the charge that a "king" or "governor" was proposed, the idea was advanced to intrust the executive with power and then hold him responsible for it; as to the self-assumed high moral stand taken by the minority, it was a fact that six of the council sat in judgment on their own acts; the charge of the minority that the proposed second House of the Legislature would be a House of Lords had no foundation; the people were to choose a legislative council from the same people that were represented in the lower House, and these members were to be elected by the same voters; the minority wilfully misrepresented the purpose of the majority; the minority offered the plan of electing the governor by the people; there could certainly be no objection to intrusting the election of the chief magistrate to voters of the State. The "Candid Examination" goes on to defend the ideas of the majority respecting the veto power, the appointing power, the election of justices of the peace, etc.

The present government of Pennsylvania, it declares, is very expensive and inefficient. By adopting the bicameral plan the interests of the State may be as fairly attended to and with far greater economy than is possible at present. The alterations proposed by the majority are designed to make the constitution of Pennsylvania like those of our neighboring States. They have a governor and a legislative branch of two Houses; but none of them contains a "king" or a "House of Lords." It is a matter of the utmost importance that a convention be called to consider the amending of the constitution.[1]

This "Candid Examination" was followed by "Remarks on the Powers of the Council of Censors,"[2] setting forth that the council did not equitably represent the State, and that, as constituted, one-fifth of the State might really bind

[1] *Pennsylvania Gazette*, No. 2800, February 11, 1784.
[2] Ibid., No. 2802, February 25, 1784.

four-fifths ; that the matter of inquiring as to the collection
of taxes and the best use of public money should really be
done by the Executive Council or by a standing committee
of the General Assembly; that seven years is too long to
wait, as defaulters might escape; that the council is power-
less to compel the General Assembly to repeal unjust laws ;
the council has no power to inflict punishment commensurate
with crimes committed; with so long a time (seven years)
between sessions, persons censured may be dead, or may
have run away; the requirement of a two-thirds vote of the
council to call a convention to amend the constitution is
absurd and tyrannical, for one-eighth of the State as represented might bind seven-eighths; that it is difficult to get
at the collective opinions of a community so represented;
the censors usurp a right contrary to the ninth article of
the Bill of Rights, by confining periods for amending the
constitution to any one term; reviewing the constitution
once in seven years tends to create a septennial convulsion—
stability would thus be lost; if the people are happy, they
ought not to be disturbed every seven years; if unhappy,
they ought not to wait so long; that the Council of Censors
is absurd, dangerous, tyrannical, and unnecessary; it is too
expensive; other States have no such provision, and Pennsylvania's position among them is lowered by this provision.

When the Council of Censors resumed its duties after the
adjournment, it proceeded (August 16) to take up the report
of the committee appointed to consider whether the constitution had been preserved inviolate in every part, a report
which had been laid on the table on January 17.[1]

The report set forth that in view of the insidious attacks
made upon the constitution it was the belief of the committee that the instrument in question is clear in its principles, accurate in its forms, consistent in its several parts,
and worthy the veneration of the people of Pennsylvania.
The committee then proceeded to consider infractions of
the constitution in detail, and finally resolved, September
16, " that there does not appear to this council an absolute

[1] " Proceedings," pp. 83, 84.

necessity to call a convention to alter or explain or amend the constitution."[1] The report was adopted by a vote of fourteen to eight, showing that the radical party was now in the majority.

That this vote was somewhat indicative of the sentiment of the State on this question one may judge from the facts that a petition of eighteen thousand citizens had been sent to the Council of Censors requesting them not to change the constitution,[2] and that in the bye-election held in Philadelphia City to fill the vacancy occasioned by the resignation of Miles, a conservative, George Bryan, a notorious radical, had been elected.

The shifting of the majority vote during the adjournment of the Council of Censors from the conservative to the radical wing presents several interesting features. Both parties had issued addresses; the adherents of each did not lack opportunity for knowing what was at stake. It was really the continuation of a contest which had been going on for many years. The conservatives had a majority—but not two-thirds—prior to adjournment; but at this time the council lacked five to complete its quota. After the adjournment the friends of the constitution, the radical party, polled fourteen votes as their maximum strength, a majority of the board. In the mean time the conservatives had lost Irvine, Hartley, and Miles; while the radicals had gained Bryan, Montgomery, Potter, and McLene. Only once in all the proceedings did a member vote otherwise than on strict party lines, and in this instance the constitution was not involved.

Whether the addresses of the majority and the minority had any effect in changing the sentiment of the people would be difficult to determine. It is certain, however, that everything possible was done to arouse public sentiment on both sides. Frederick Muhlenberg, in the early summer of 1784, admitted that his side was beaten, and attributed it to the " blind passion and mad party spirit of the common crowd" in electing George Bryan. He felt that if the people

[1] " Proceedings," p. 124.   [2] Ibid., p. 123.

of the State had been equitably represented, particularly if
the "intelligent part of the people" could have had a voice,
their judgment would have favored the amendments.[1]

Joseph Reed felt that a mistake was made at the outset
by proposing to make too many changes in the constitution.
His view was that if only a few changes had been proposed,
there might have been some reasonable hope of carrying
a proposition for a Constitutional Convention through the
Council of Censors by the requisite two-thirds vote. A
moderate course would have tended to conciliate, and would
have brought some measure of success in remedying some
of the defects of the constitution,—for it certainly had
defects.[2] George Bryan came in for a series of attacks in
the *Pennsylvania Gazette*,[3] in one of which he is characterized as the "*spem gregis*" and " Censor-General of Pennsylvania."[4]

It seems that the cause of the conservative party was
really hopeless from the outset, and that it grew more so as
the agitation increased. There was no question as to the
fact that the constitution was defective, but there was a re-
luctance to making radical changes; and, moreover, it had
not then occurred to the people as a whole how cumbrous
their machinery was for changing the fundamental law.
Then, too, controversies that dated back to the time when
the proprietary government was in power were not entirely
healed—all these elements had their influence in keeping
the party lines rigid in the Council of Censors.

On September 24 the censors made their address to the
people and on the 25th adjourned.[5] The address to the
people set forth that although there doubtless were defects
in the constitution, yet it had been decided that there was
no absolute necessity for calling a convention, and partly for
the reason that the censors could not agree upon the

---

[1] PENNA. MAG., Vol. XII. p. 199.
[2] Letter of Joseph Reed to William Bradford, May 2, 1784, " Life and
Correspondence of Joseph Reed," Vol. II. p. 411.
[3] *Pennsylvania Gazette*, Nos. 2829, 2830, 2831, 2833, 2834.
[4] Ibid., No. 2829, August 25, 1784.   [5] " Proceedings," p. 128.

changes needed; that the censors had set forth in detail the infringements upon the constitution which they had observed; that they regretted the lack of unanimity in the council and regarded it as unfortunate that the question of calling a convention should have come before the censors so early in their sessions; and that the censors had not attempted to interpret the constitution further than to explain their view of certain sections to show wherein they had been violated.[1]

This address was approved by a vote of twelve to nine, and the work of the Council of Censors of Pennsylvania for 1783–84 was ended.

VIII. PENNSYLVANIA: THE CONVENTION OF 1789–90.

As the Council of Censors was to be elected once in seven years, the second council for Pennsylvania would have been elected in 1790. Following closely upon the heels of the Council of Censors of 1783–84 came the discontent with the old Confederation and the framing and adoption of the Federal Constitution. Pennsylvania ratified this instrument, which provided for amendments in a more equitable manner than by a Council of Censors.

The change in sentiment thus evinced bore fruit in a proposition presented to the Legislature on March 24, 1789, to appeal to the people for their judgment as to calling a Constitutional Convention; if they concurred in this, then a convention was to be chosen. The House passed these resolutions by a vote of forty-one to seventeen.

A dissentient report was made by sixteen members, among whom was that James McLene who had, as a member of the Council of Censors, voted to preserve the integrity of the constitution in 1776. Their main line of argument was that if changes were to be made they should be made by a Council of Censors, for any other way was not in accordance with the constitution and might lead to a revolution; the present form of government was not too expensive,—indeed, not as expensive as those of sister States;

[1] "Proceedings," pp. 127, 128.

and, while it might be shown that there are defects in our
constitution, it should be replied that it has stood the test
of time; but if it were to be amended it should be done in
the way provided by the constitution.[1]

On September 15 of the same year the General Assembly
in committee of the whole considered the matter of calling
a convention to alter and amend the constitution, and reported to the House in favor of the measure. The report
set forth that it was believed that the people desired this,
" in preference to the mode by the Council of Censors,
which was not only unequal and unnecessarily expensive,
but too dilatory to produce the speedy and necessary alterations which the late change in the political union and the
exigencies of the State required;" that the Bill of Rights
recognized the people as possessed of all the necessary
powers in the premises; that the members of the Assembly
had mixed with the people of the State and found them de-
sirous to have a convention called; that this proceeding
was right and necessary. The report recommended that
the members of the convention be elected as the members
of the Assembly are elected and upon the same day; and
the suggestion was added that the convention should meet,
propose the needed alterations and amendments, submit
them to the people for their consideration, and then adjourn
for four months previous to the completion of their work.[2]

One member objected to the Assembly's going beyond
its powers to instruct a convention as to any details of its
duties, since this should be done by the people whom it
was to represent. The resolution for calling a convention
was passed by a vote of thirty-nine to seventeen.

Here, again, came a dissentient report by ten members,
setting forth that the Assembly had no right to call a convention; that there was no reason for such a measure; that
when a recent attempt was made to ascertain the sense of
the people as to such a measure, they were very pronounced
in opposing it, because they were satisfied with the present
constitution; that the Executive Council had not been

---

[1] " Proceedings," pp. 131–133.   [2] Ibid., 134 *et seq.*

properly consulted as to the measures proposed; that too little time was given the people to prepare for such a measure; and that this order partook of the nature of a revolution.

A correspondent of the *Gazette*, in April, declared that the choice of the State was the result of the sentiments of her citizens; that the Council of Censors that met to consider the present constitution was elected under the same vicious principle upon which our constitution was framed, " Each county, great and small, had the same number of voters, each had a vote."[1] The people of Pennsylvania had tested the Council of Censors once and had been disappointed, and for a long time no opportunity had been given the people to express their desire as to the changing of our present constitution.

Benjamin Rush, who had opposed the constitution in 1777, was still hostile to it, and urged Timothy Pickering to accept a place in the new convention. He felt that one of the greatest boons to Pennsylvania would be a convention that should change the State constitution to correspond more fully with " *the new continental wagon.*"[2] Albert Gallatin felt that the constitution ought to be changed, but he wanted it changed in the legal way, through the censors. He became, however, a member of the convention, and in after-years spoke in high terms of the character and ability of the members.[3] Charles Biddle's views were quite like those of Mr. Gallatin.[4] There was evidently a general feeling in the State that the constitution of 1776, framed in the midst of war and confusion, was not adequate to the needs of the State. The political judgment of Pennsylvania had outgrown it.

The convention for revising the constitution met at Philadelphia on November 24, 1789, in accordance with

---

[1] *Pennsylvania Gazette*, April 29, 1789.
[2] Letter of Benjamin Rush, Pickering and Upham's " Life of Pickering," Vol. II. p. 428.
[3] Adams's " Life of Gallatin," pp. 79–81.
[4] " Autobiography of Charles Biddle."

the vote of the General Assembly; but, no quorum being present, it adjourned to the 25th, when it organized, with Thomas Mifflin as president. On December 21 the committee appointed to bring in a draft of a constitution presented a report embracing substantially the points which had been rejected by the Council of Censors in 1783-84. Among these were the bicameral Legislature, a single executive to be elected by the people, and a qualified veto power to be vested in the governor.

Article IX., Section II., contained all that the committee had to offer on the subject of amending the constitution: [1]

"That all power is inherent in the people, and all free governments are founded on their authority, and instituted for their peace, safety, and happiness: For the advancement of these ends, they have, at all times, an unalienable and indefeasible right to alter, reform, or abolish their government, in such manner as they may think proper."

The Council of Censors was ignored, the people having evidently become wearied with so unwieldy a piece of political machinery, and the more so because its weakness became more manifest as the people came to see and appreciate their needs.

The reason why the people of Pennsylvania had borne with the constitution of 1776 and the Council of Censors—indeed, their very origin—lay in the fact that the State had been for years divided into two hostile political camps. The censors and the constitution of 1776 were the means whereby the radical party hoped to keep their own rights from invasion by the conservatives, who had been so powerful in the proprietary colony.

The Revolutionary feelings were still in evidence when the Council of Censors met in 1783-84; but during the next seven years a change had come. The Rousseau views which had evidently prompted Paine, Matlack, and Cannon to their work had quietly yielded to the milder influence of John Locke. The Confederation had proved to be a failure. The thirteen independent States had united to form "a more perfect union."

[1] "Proceedings," p. 303.

The United States had ventured to trust the execution of its laws to a single executive properly checked by the other departments of the government. Philadelphia was the seat of the convention in which this work was done; Pennsylvania was the Keystone State; she felt the changes that had come about in the other commonwealths. In 1789 the people were ready to move forward, and the new constitution was the exponent of this progress. Enough had been done when it was declared that the people were the rightful repositories of the political power of the State, and that they could of right decide the times and the manner of altering or amending their fundamental law.

IX. The Significance of the Council of Censors in Pennsylvania.

Pennsylvania enjoyed a unique position among her sister colonies from her geographical position and from the fact that her proprietary government continued down to the Revolution, a fact which contributed not a little to the political bitterness which was manifested so forcibly and frequently while the constitution of 1776 was in force.

This constitution was a step into the darkness of experiment. There were no models of popular government to take pattern by; hence the models of Greece and Rome were studied in the light of Locke, Montesquieu, and Rousseau.

The fatal stumbling-block seems to have been found in the plan for giving the people supervision over their government and its officials.

The constitution of 1776 seems to have been the advance wave of the levelling influence of the American Revolution. The social and political condition of Pennsylvania was ready for this change, and the commotion which followed the making of the new constitution was simply a preparation for the more stable form which was sure to follow.

The Council of Censors of 1783–84 was elected, and its work was given to the people, but the constitution was continued. Faulty and defective as it was, the people of Pennsylvania were not to be dragooned into more radical changes.

Within the following seven years thirteen independent republics laid aside the treaty or Confederation by which they were loosely held together and merged their sovereignty in a national government.

The fundamental law of this nation provided a means always accessible to the people for altering or amending this great instrument, which was the product of the ablest statesmanship of the States. While the influence of this great work was fresh in the minds of the people of Pennsylvania, and just on the eve of the election of a second Council of Censors, her General Assembly touched the pulse of public sentiment and, finding the people ready for the movement, called a convention which framed a constitution on better lines and with better adjusted political machinery. In the executive, in the Legislature, and in the method of amending the constitution the principal changes were made ; and the great principle was laid down, and has ever since been maintained, that it is in the province of the people of the State to decide the time and the method of changing the fundamental law in a popular government.

THE COUNCIL OF CENSORS OF VERMONT.([1])

The territory now included in the state of Vermont was originally claimed by New Hampshire and New York.

In response to a letter from Governor Wentworth of New Hampshire to Governor Clinton of New York, relative to determining the boundary between New York and New Hampshire west of the Connecticut River, the letter dated at Portsmouth, N. H., November 17, 1749, Governor Clinton replied that the province of New York was bounded on the east by the Connecticut River agreeably to the grant made by Charles II. of England to his brother James, Duke of York. ([2])

On January 3d, of this year, Governor Wentworth gave a grant of a township in the south-western part of what is now Vermont. This was named Bennington, and was the earliest grant made by New Hampshire. Between this time and December, 1764, one hundred and thirty town grants and six private grants had been made by New Hampshire. New York did not recognize the legality of these grants and efforts were made to place and retain them under the power of New York. Governor Tryon offered rewards for the arrest of Ethan Allen and others, because of their prominence in resisting the claims of New York. The Vermonters at once banded together to protect the towns of the New Hampshire Grants from interference on the part of New York.

In March, 1775, occurred the riot at Westminster, and after this the towns east of the Green Mountains united in

([1]) The portion of this paper which follows was read before the Vermont Historical Society at Montpelier on October 18, 1898, and is here reprinted from the Proceedings of that Society, by its kind permission.

([2]) Slade, Vermont State Papers, p. 9, et seq.

resistance to the claims of New York, and at a meeting in
Westminster, April 11, 1775, a resolution to this effect was
adopted. (¹)

Before July 4, 1776, the citizens of the New Hampshire Grants were mostly loyal to Great Britain; after this
date they claimed to be independent, and called a meeting
of citizens at Dorset, July 24. An adjournment was taken
to September 25, when delegates numbering fifty-one and
representing thirty-five towns, met at Cephas Kent's in Dorset.(²) At this meeting it was resolved " to declare the New
Hampshire Grants a free and separate district." This
vote passed without a dissenting voice. The meeting
further resolved as follows : (³)

" We, the subscribers, inhabitants of that district of
land commonly called and known by the name of New
Hampshire Grants, being legally delegated and authorized
to transact the public and political affairs of the aforesaid
district for ourselves and constituents, do solemnly covenant
and engage, that, for the time being, we will strictly and
religiously adhere to the several resolves of this or a future
convention, constituted on said district by the free voice of
the friends to American liberties, which shall not be repug-
nant to the resolves of the honorable the Continental Congress relative to the cause of America."

This Convention adjourned to meet at Westminster
January 15, 1777. At this meeting it was voted, " That
the district of territory comprehending and usually known
by the name and description of the New Hampshire
grants," be a new and separate state, " forever hereafter to
be called, known and distinguished by the name of New
Connecticut." (⁴) On January 22, the Convention adjourned
to meet at Windsor the first Wednesday in June.(⁵)

(¹) Slade, State Papers, p. 60.
(²) State Papers, p. 66.
(³) State Papers, p. 67.
(⁴) See Hiland Hall's Early Vermont, pp. 239, 497–500.
(⁵) State Papers, p. 79.

This Convention met according to adjournment on the first Wednesday in June and voted that a committee be appointed to draft a constitution; "and a resolution was adopted, recommending to each town to elect delegates to meet in convention, at Windsor, on the second day of July following." July 2, the delegates came together and proceeded to consider the draft of the constitution proposed. The constitution was read paragraph by paragraph and adopted without referring it to the people for ratification. There were two reasons for this: 1, It was definitely understood by the towns that the delegates chosen for this convention were vested with all necessary powers for framing a constitution; and, 2, Burgoyne's invasion made it impossible to call the citizens together for purposes of ratification. Moreover, Pennsylvania had adopted a constitution the previous year without ratification, and besides, the theory of popular government was not so far advanced then as to disturb public judgment over such an omission, and particularly since the power that made, was able to unmake, the constitution at will.

In this Convention it was voted that the first election under the constitution should be held in December, 1777, and that the legislature should meet at Bennington the following January.

This Convention had appointed a Committee of Safety as a part of its work, to provide for the defence of the State. Ira Allen, who was to have the constitution printed at Hartford, Connecticut, for distribution to the citizens of Vermont in season for the December election, was unable to carry out his plans, so the Committee of Safety summoned the Convention to meet again December 24, 1777. ([1]) The Convention met, made some changes in the constitution, changed the date of the new election to the first Tuesday in March, 1778, and voted that the Legislature assemble

([1]) State Papers, p. 80.

the second Thursday of the same month at Windsor. The
Legislature met accordingly in Windsor, adopted the Constitution and proceeded with the legislative work of the
State. Bennington was the only town in the State that
opposed the adoption of the Constitution without its being
previously ratified by the people; this objection was drop-
ped.

The source of the first Vermont Constitution can readily
be traced. At the Westminster Convention, January 15,
1777, Dr. Jonas Fay, Thomas Chittenden, Heman Allen
and Reuben Jones brought in a draft of a petition to Congress relative to the territory of Vermont, based on her
declaration of independence and the free action of her citizens in convention assembled. This committee went to
Philadelphia and presented their petition to Congress; but
in the meantime they fell in (¹) with the "red republicans"
who had been instrumental in drawing up the draft of
the Pennsylvania Constitution the year previous. Dr.
Thomas Young, James Cannon, and Timothy Matlack were
leaders (²) of the radicals in Pennsylvania, and Dr. Young
was an old acquaintance of Ethan Allen's while the latter
resided in Connecticut. Dr. Young suggested the name of
Vermont and in a public letter dated April 11, 1777, and
published in a Philadelphia newspaper, he urged the Vermonters to adopt a State organization and seek admission
to Congress. As a matter of fact the Constitution of
Vermont was an exact copy of that of Pennsylvania, with a
few minor changes. Among its provisions was that of providing a council of thirteen censors to be elected once in
seven years, to determine whether the laws were duly executed, whether they were constitutional, and whether there
were need of a revision of the Constitution. This section,
Section XLV., read as follows:

(¹)   Ira Allen's History of Vermont, p. 86.
(²)   Hiland Hall's History of Vermont, pp. 497–500.

" In order that the freedom of this commonwealth may be preserved inviolate, forever, there shall be chosen, by ballot, by the Freemen of this State, on the last Wednesday in March, in the year one thousand seven hundred and eighty-five, and on the last Wednesday in March, in every seven years thereafter, thirteen persons, who shall be chosen in the same manner the Council is chosen—except they shall not be out of the Council or General Assembly—to be called the Council of Censors; who shall meet together on the first Wednesday of June next ensuing their election; the majority of whom shall be a quorum in every case, except as to calling a Convention, in which two-thirds of the whole number elected shall agree; and whose duty it shall be to enquire whether the Constitution has been preserved inviolate in every part; and whether the legislative and executive branches of government have performed their duty as guardians of the people; or assumed to themselves, or exercised, other or greater powers, than they are entitled by the Constitution.

" They are also to enquire whether the public taxes have been justly laid and collected, in all parts of this Commonwealth—in what manner the public monies have been disposed of, and whether the laws have been duly executed.

" For these purposes they shall have power to send for persons, papers and records; they shall have authority to pass public censures—to order impeachments, and to recommend to the legislature the repealing such laws as appear to them to have been enacted contrary to the principles of the Constitution. These powers they shall continue to have, for and during the space of one year from the day of their election, and no longer. The said Council of Censors shall also have power to call a Convention, to meet within two years after their sitting, if there appears to them an absolute necessity of amending any article of this Constitution which may be defective—explaining such as may be thought

not clearly expressed, and adding such as are necessary for
the preservation of the rights and happiness of the people;
but the articles to be amended, and the amendments proposed, and such articles as are proposed to be added or
abolished, shall be promulgated at least six months before
the day appointed for the election of such convention, for
the previous consideration of the people, that they may have
an opportunity of instructing their delegates on the subject." (¹)

The Constitution of Vermont was launched upon a
stormy sea. The colonists were in the midst of a war for
their independence; her territory had already been invaded
and made the scene of battle. Nor was this all her trouble;
for New York was pressing her claims to the territory
known as the New Hampshire Grants.

At the session of the Legislature held in Bennington
on February 11, 1779, there was a formal ratification of the
Constitution and a declaration that this instrument with
such alterations or amendments as should be made in the
future should be "forever considered, held, and maintained,
as part of the laws of this State." (²)   At the June session
held at Windsor in 1782, there was a second formal ratification (³) which recognized the 45th section of the Constitution as providing the means for further altering or
amending the Constitution.

At first the people of Vermont seem to have regarded
the Constitution as of no more importance than an ordinary
act of the legislature.(⁴)   That the importance of the Constitution as the fundamental law of the State was a matter
of growth in the minds of the people of Vermont is borne
out by the fact that it was not until November 2, 1796, that

(¹) Slade, State Papers, p. 255.
(²) Slade, State Papers, p. 288.
(³) Slade, State Papers, p. 449.
(⁴) Judge Chipman's Memoirs of Thomas Chittenden, Chap.
     V.

the legislature declared the Constitution to be the "supreme law of the land."([1])

That this view should have been taken seems reasonable from the nature of the case. Here was an independent community, lately under an exacting monarchy, with its integrity threatened by the demands of a sister commonwealth, now attempting to govern itself by its own laws. The people felt their way until their constitutional light became bright enough for them to proceed with a full measure of conscious strength.

The Earlier Councils of Censors and Conventions, 1785–1836.

The first Council of Censors met in 1785 and held three sessions; one at Norwich in June, one at Windsor in September, and one at Bennington in February, 1786. ([2]) This Council renewed the legislation of the previous seven years, proposed a number of amendments to the Constitution, and voted that a convention should be called to consider them.

The convention met at Manchester on the last Thursday in June, 1786, and ratified some of the amendments proposed by the Council. ([3]) Among these the most important seem to be these: that the legislative, executive, and judiciary departments should be kept distinct: that the people "by their legal representatives" have the sole right of governing and regulating the police affairs of the State: and that the fourteenth section of the Frame of Government should so read as to confer upon the Governor and Council a qualified veto power, and the power to propose amendments to bills passed by the Assembly, with the further provision that if the Assembly should not concur in these amendments then the Governor and Council could suspend

([1]) Poore's Charters and Constitutions, p. 1875.
([2]) Slade, State Papers, p. 511.
([3]) Records of the Governor and Council, Vol. I, pp. 84-85. Chipman's Memoirs of Thomas Chittenden, Chap. VIII.

the passage of these bills until the next session of the Legislature. (¹) We believe this to have been the first instance in constitutional history of a written constitution being amended by representatives of the people and at the command of the people.

Vermont was admitted to the Union by the Act of Congress of March 6, 1791, with its Constitution as it had been amended by the first Council of Censors and the Manchester Convention of 1786 and ratified (²) by the state legislature of 1787. Hitherto Vermont had enjoyed the unique distinction of being an independent commonwealth, bound to the Union by no ties save those of patriotic sympathy. She had established and maintained a government, had resisted invasion, had assisted in carrying on the Revolution, and had patiently waited for the opportunity to yield her independence to the end that she might enjoy the privileges and share the burdens of the federal union.

In 1792 another Council met and proposed several radical changes. It was proposed that the Legislature should be made bi-cameral, a Senate taking the place of the "Executive Council"; each town was to have one representative in the lower house provided it had forty families, otherwise two or more towns together having forty families could send one; the Senate was to be based on proportional representation from the counties. (³) In its address to the people, in 1792, the Council said: "In examining the proceedings of the legislative and executive departments of this government during the last septenary, we are happy to find no proceedings which we judge unconstitutional or deserving

---

(¹) Mr. Huse, Revised Laws of Vermont, edition of 1881, p. 57, thinks that the Council may be said practically to have effected a general revision of the Constitution in respect to details and expression.

(²) Governor and Council of Vermont, Vol. III. p. 133. Chipman's Memoirs of Thomas Chittenden, Chap. V.

(³) Thompson's Gazetteer, p. 125; Slade, State Papers, p. 545-6.

of censure." (¹)   The Convention met at Windsor, July 4-9, 1793, but none of the proposed amendments were adopted. The people of Vermont were slow to adopt the recommendations of the Council of Censors.   They had followed Pennsylvania in adopting their Constitution with its single legislative branch and Council of Censors.   Pennsylvania had now discarded these two institutions, but conservative Vermont held steadily to her adopted plan.

Even at this early day, however, an idea had begun to take root that the Council of Censors was not worthy of the full measure of confidence which it seemed to possess at first.   Dr. Samuel Williams, writing in 1806, in speaking of this body declared that an experience of thirty years had disappointed the people as to the benefits derived from the Council of Censors.   He complained of the manner of their election, that it was liable to partisan control, that their proceedings were often characterized by " prejudice, partiality, contracted views and want of comprehension. The assembly often pay but little regard to their decisions and the people still less."   He added, " Time and experience will determine what is wanted in this part of our Constitution." (²)

The third Council of Censors met in February, 1800, but they prepared no amendments to the Constitution. They recommended, however, that the Legislature repeal the act of October 6, 1796, empowering the supreme court judges to deprive a man of his right to vote " for any evil action which shall render him notoriously scandalous." (³) They also recommended the repeal of the act of October 25, 1797, relating to the support of the gospel, except the first and last sections, as contrary to the third section of the bill of rights in the Constitution.   They also took note of

(¹)   Proceedings of Council of Censors, Printed by Anthony Haswell in Rutland, 1792. Bound volume in State Library, Montpelier, Vt.

(²)   Williams' History of Vermont, II., pp. 400–401.

(³)   Address of Council of Censors, Vermont State Library, p. 11.

a matter relative to a sheriff's charging constructive mileage in serving court papers. The case is not without interest. The Council of Censors ordered the Legislature to impeach William Coley, high sheriff of Bennington county, for taking illegal fees for summoning the grand and petit jurors to serve before the supreme court at Manchester at the February and June terms, 1798. It should be stated that the supreme court judges had approved his charges. The Legislature took the matter up and October 26, 1799, went into a committee of the whole to consider the question set forth by the Council of Censors. This resulted in the appointment of a committee to take up the case of Sheriff Coley; and, November 2, 1799, Richard Hurd reported for the committee, finding that Coley's charges for service of venires on the jurors in question amounted to $38.27, that the judges regarded it a high price, that they audited it on Coley's representation that he had been obliged to go into several towns to summon the jurors. ([1]) The committee further reported that as the law required a venire for fifteen jurors, for each petit jury, it was presumable that that number was summoned; they found that six others were summoned; that he made two journeys to Dorset and one to Sandgate in quest of jurors. The committee carefully considered his statements and found that he was entitled to $39.23, a sum larger than he actually charged by $1.06. It appeared by the report of this committee that Mr. Coley did the work above referred to and personally attended the two sessions of court, and carried one prisoner from Bennington to Manchester—receiving for all the sum of $53.65. ([2]) The Legislature ratified this report and the order of the Council of Censors was dismissed.

At this time a committee was appointed to report what changes should be made in the " Fee-Bill " and, three days

([1]) Address of Council of Censors, 1800, pp. 12–13.
([2]) Address of Council of Censors, 1800, p. 13.

later, November 5, 1799, Mr. Josiah Wright for the committee reported as follows:

"That upon examining the law, [the committee] are of opinion it cannot be construed so as to give an officer more than six cents a mile for actual travel for serving any one process, although several persons may be named in it, and served on the same, except it be a forced construction. Therefore, are of opinion that no alteration ought to be made."

The Council of Censors took up this work of the legislature, examined it critically, showed the infelicity in allowing constructive mileage to Mr. Coley and later affirming a principle opposed to this construction of the law. This case and several other important matters were published in the *Address to the People*, and distributed over the State.

There is a peculiar interest in this case because it sheds light on the principles which underlay the structure of the Vermont commonwealth. No one could affirm that Sheriff Coley was becoming a plutocrat when his fees for an entire year were only $53.65; nor can one fail to admire the fearless action of the Censors who bravely examined every detail of the case and laid it before the people of the State. Here reappears the spirit of John Hampden who will not yield a principle even though the amount at issue be but twenty shillings.

The fourth Council of Censors met at Woodstock in December, 1806. No amendments to the Constitution were proposed; but, in the address to the people, they suggested that the Legislature should change several laws. One was the act of November 3, 1800, in support of the gospel, the objection being that it was contrary to the third section of the bill of rights; the other law was the one that required an alien or stranger to remain three years in the State before he could acquire the privileges of citizenship, the change suggested making it apply to all citizens alike, native or adopted, agreeably to the thirty-ninth section of the Constitution. (¹)

The fifth Council of Censors met at Montpelier, June 2-4, and October 14—November 1, 1813, and at Middlebury, January 19-24, 1814. (²) This time a large number of amendments were proposed, but of these we only mention the most important. The plan for a Senate to take the place of the Executive Council that was proposed in 1792 and failed of ratification by the convention, was now renewed with several suggested changes. It was to consist of twenty-four members apportioned among the counties according to population ; the term of office was to be three years, one-third retiring each year. The judges of the Supreme Court were to serve during good behavior subject to removal from office on a two-thirds vote of both houses of the Legislature. It was proposed, also, that an amendment be added prohibiting the suspension of the writ of *habeas corpus* under any circumstances.

No changes had been made in the constitution for twenty-one years, and none had been suggested by the Council of Censors for fourteen years. A strong effort was now made to bring the Vermont Constitution up to a point of excellence that should cause it to rank with those of the sister states. On February 22, 1814, Charles Marsh, Esq., delivered an address (³) at Norwich on the occasion of the celebration of Washington's birthday. His theme was the proposed amendments. He argued in favor of a senate to check the legislation of the lower house ; he would give the judiciary greater independence by extending the tenure of office of the judges. He disapproved of the idea of electing the executive council on a general ticket because men would be obliged to vote for men with whom they were

(¹) Proceedings of Council of Censors, Vermont State Library.

(²) Journal of Council of Censors, Vermont State Library.

(³) An Essay on the Amendments Proposed : Hanover, N. H. ; Printed by Charles Spear. Pamphlet of 21 pp., Vermont State Library.

not acquainted. Representation in the senate would, he asserted, secure the election of men who were known by their neighbors. He cited the fickleness of France as shown in her national assembly, and endorsed the views of Washington that the salaries of judges should not be diminished during continuance in office.

The Convention called to consider the proposed amendments met at Montpelier June 7, 1814, and completed their work June 9. Not an amendment suggested by the Council of Censors was endorsed. Twenty-three amendments were negatived without a dissenting vote; the proposition for a senate commanded twenty votes in its favor, while one hundred and eighty-eight voted against it. The amendment prohibiting the suspension of the writ of *habeas corpus* polled the strongest vote in its favor of any amendment, but it, too, went down with fifty-one yeas in its favor to one hundred and fifty-six nays opposed to its ratification. (¹) The sentiments of Mr. Marsh were evidently not shared by a majority of the citizens of Vermont, for the people were not ready for these advanced steps in political life.

The sixth Council of Censors met at Montpelier and held three sessions: June 7–8, October 17–27, 1820; and March 15–26, 1821. Five amendments (²) were proposed and a Constitutional Convention was called. The amendments in brief were to vest the legislative power in the Executive Council and House of Representatives; to apportion the representatives so that there should be two representatives for every 2,000 inhabitants; to prevent any judge of the supreme court from holding any other state or town office; to vest the executive power in a governor and lieutenant-governor; and to make the period of service of the supreme court judges seven years. It further provided for

(¹) Constitutional Conventions of Vermont, Vermont State Library.

(²) Journal of Council of Censors, Vermont State Library.

the removal of the judges by impeachment, should an occasion arise for such a step.

The Constitutional Convention met at Montpelier, February 21–23, 1822, to consider the amendments proposed by the Censors. It sat only two days and adjourned without date. The first amendment was defeated with no one to support it; the vote on the second stood fourteen yeas, two hundred and two nays; the third stood yeas ninety-three, nays one hundred and twenty-one; the fourth was discarded but the vote was not given; the fifth stood yeas nineteen, nays one hundred and ninety-three. (¹) Not an amendment was ratified, and Vermont's fundamental law stood just where it did when she entered the Union in 1791.

The seventh Council of Censors met at Montpelier for two sessions—June 6–8, and October 15–26; and at Burlington November 26–30, 1827. It proposed three amendments(²) and called a Constitutional Convention. For the fourth time a Senate was suggested as a second branch of the legislature, a qualified veto power was given to the governor, and it was further proposed that the privileges of citizenship should be denied to foreigners until they should be naturalized under the laws of the United States.

The Convention met at Montpelier June 26–28, 1828. It passed the third amendment, as to naturalization as a requisite for citizenship in the State, by a vote of one hundred and thirty-four for to ninety-two against the measure; but the first two were defeated, the vote on the Senate and veto power standing yeas forty-seven, nays one hundred and eighty-two.(³)

(¹) Vermont Constitutional Conventions, Vermont State Library ; Thompson's Vermont, Part II, p. 126.

(²) Journal of Council of Censors, Vermont State Library.

(³) Vermont Constitutional Conventions, Vermont State Library ; Thompson's Vermont, Part II, pp. 125–127.

The eighth Council of Censors met at Montpelier for two sessions, June 4-6, and October 15-24, 1834, and at Middlebury for the third session, January 7-16, 1835. It proposed nineteen amendments to the Constitution and called a Constitutional Convention.

The Convention met at Montpelier January 6-14, 1836, and adopted twelve of the amendments proposed by the Censors. Among the most important were the measure providing a Senate to replace the Executive Council, as a second branch of the Legislature, apportioning the Senators among the counties according to their population, giving it sole power to try impeachments, vesting the executive power in a governor and lieutenant-governor, prohibiting the suspension of the writ of *habeas corpus* for any reason, and providing for the election of certain officials by counties and probate districts.[1] There is a certain interest in considering the vote on the amendment providing for a Senate. The proposition was now for a fifth time before a Vermont Constitutional Convention.[2] Judge Chipman[3] had addressed the Convention the first day of the session, and yet when this amendment was reached it was ratified by the slender majority of three, the yeas being one hundred and sixteen and the nays one hundred and thirteen. A motion to reconsider this vote was made and lost by a vote of one hundred and ten to one hundred and nineteen.[4] This action abolished the Executive Council and placed Vermont on a plane with the other States in that her Legislature was now bi-cameral.

The Censors had suggested the amendment in 1792, in 1814, in 1820, and in 1827, and each time the Convention following the Censors had vetoed the measure. Perhaps

[1]   Journal of Council of Censors, Vermont State Library.

[2]   Vermont Constitutional Conventions, Vermont State Library.

[3]   Judge Chipman's Address, Vermont State Library.

[4]   Vermont Constitutional Conventions.

there is no more striking illustration in Vermont's constitutional history, to show how the radical or progressive ideas of the Censors were sent to the rear by the conservative constitutional conventions, than the time and persistency required to establish a Senate in place of the Executive Council. It was adopted forty-four years after it was first proposed, and after it had been proposed and defeated four times.

The Later Councils of Censors and Conventions, 1842—1869.

The ninth (¹) Council of Censors held three sessions: two in Montpelier and one in Burlington. They proposed seven amendments and called a Convention to meet in Montpelier in January, 1842. The amendments proposed failed of adoption, not one passing by the requisite vote of the convention. It may be interesting to note the nature of some of these as proposed by the Censors, viz : that the general State election be held the second Tuesday in October annually forever ; that the legislature meet on the first Thursday in June each year until by law some other day should be selected ; that the Senate be divided into classes, one-third retiring each year, the senatorial term being three years ; that sheriffs and high bailiffs be elected by the freemen of the counties ; that justices of the Supreme Court be elected for seven years, subject to removal by impeachment brought by a two-thirds vote of each branch of the legislature. The Council of Censors was unwilling to have the method of suggesting amendments to the Constitution transferred from the Council of Censors to the legislature. They proposed, however, to give the people the privilege of voting directly on amendments, either to adopt or reject. In this case each voter could register his opinion on the amendments proposed.

(¹) Thompson's Vermont, Part II, pp. 125-127 ; Niles' Register, Vol. 63, Nov. 19, 1842.

The tenth Council met in 1848–9 and the constitutional convention which passed upon its work met in Montpelier, Jan. 2–14, 1850. It ratified amendments to the Constitution to the effect that the people should elect the assistant judges, sheriffs, high bailiffs and judges of probate; that justices of the peace should be elected by the people, and that senators, to be eligible, should be at least thirty years old.

The eleventh Council of Censors met at Montpelier in October 1855, and proposed a series of amendments, none of which were ratified. Some of these propositions were for biennial sessions of the legislature and two-year periods for State officers; that the house of representatives be composed of 150 members to be apportioned among the counties, each county to have at least two, the counties being divided into districts on an equitable basis; that the Senate should be composed of four members from each county, the senatorial term to be four years, with the body divided into two classes, one-half retiring biennially; that the judges of the Supreme Court be elected for six years, one-third retiring each two years; that a constitutional convention be composed of ninety delegates, apportioned among the counties, each having at least two, the rest being apportioned among the counties according to population.

It seems strange that not one of these proposed amendments was ratified. One may reasonably infer that the Councils of Censors were more nearly abreast of the times in governmental affairs, while the constitutional conventions represented the conservatism of the State.

In 1862 the twelfth Council of Censors was chosen. It met but proposed no amendments. At this time the Civil War was in progress, and the larger danger of disunion overshadowed any defects which might otherwise have been found in the commonwealth's fundamental law.

The thirteenth and, as it proved, the final Council of Censors met in Montpelier, June 2, 1869. It was composed of thirteen members : Henry Lane, J. B. Hollister, William Harmon, Jasper Rand, H. Henry Powers, J. R. Cleveland, Nathaniel W. French, Charles C. Dewey, Charles K. Field, Timothy P. Redfield, Charles Reed, Joseph W. Colburn, and Jonathan Ross. The Censors met in the Senate Chamber at Montpelier, June 2, 1869. They held three sessions : July 2-4, July 27 to August 6, and October 19-22.

At the afternoon session of June 2, Mr. J. W. Colburn introduced a resolution that a committee of three should be appointed to consider a plan of changing the method of amending the Constitution " so as to refer to legislative action for propositions, and refer directly to the people for a final decision, as more appropriate and less expensive than the present system and more in accordance with republican ideas and democratic equality." On that committee were appointed Mr. Colburn, Mr. Lane, Mr. Powers. Saturday, July 31, Mr. Colburn for the minority of the committee begged leave to report in favor of abolishing the Council of Censors for reasons which in substance are as follows:

There were good reasons for having the Council when it was adopted, but these reasons exist no longer. (¹) Then we had few newspapers, few books, few schools. It was felt to be unsafe to entrust the amending of the Constitution directly to the people. We adopted the present system from Pennsylvania—one used by no other State and discarded by Pennsylvania after giving it a brief trial. Since 1850 the people have taken little interest in amendments to the Constitution ; not one in ten seemed to understand the Constitution or how it was amended ; and a system so little understood should not exist longer. To-day the people are better educated, more capable of judging on constitutional matters ; hence it would be well, once in ten years, to submit to them the proposition whether the Constitution needs

(¹) Journal of Council of Censors, Montpelier, 1869.

revision. When our government was organized we had two great parties—" Federal" and " Republican." "The former took the ground that the people were not to be trusted with the powers of self-government; the latter contended that they were safe depositories of this power." (¹) The old Federal party has gone, but the relic of Federalism remains in this antiquated custom of having a Council of Censors ; and this is left only because of the apathy of the people; for " the people know and care but little about the changes of their Constitution." Does some one argue that the Council has other duties besides amending the Constitution ? They are to review legislation, but in the heat of the War of 1812 they censured some acts of the legislature. " It undid nothing, it righted nothing." Its action came too late and was not effective. The people themselves remedied the evil legislation by failure to re-elect the members in question, and this remedy is always with them and efficacious. The ballot-box and the Supreme Court are sufficient remedies,—let these be used. This machinery is cumbersome, antiquated and has been almost useless for three-fourths of a century. The Council of 1855 proposed amendments, but the Convention following in its wake voted them down ; but all this was expensive. Mischief is liable to be done in such ways. The small towns are guarded in their rights, each one having a unit of representation ; this they can not lose, for they will not yield it. A two-thirds vote of the Legislature once in ten years will correct any evils that may arise. The argument of " let well enough alone" is not germane to the question. We have improved implements in agriculture and mechanical lines, then why not improve governmental machinery ? For the old Executive Council we substituted the Senate in 1836 and from time to time we have made other changes. We want our people to know our Constitution, to take an interest in it. Other

(¹) Journal of 1869, p. 43.

states succeed in this regard; shall Vermont be less progressive? Some one complains that the expense will be burdensome with the Legislature "continually tampering" with the business now and formerly done by the Censors; and that its sessions will be spun out to too great length. But this is lame; for it can be done only once in every decade. The session would never be delayed more than a week on this business, and the added expense is imaginary, since the Council meets once in seven years with the possibility of a constitutional convention to follow it, while the present plan is to suggest changes only once in ten years. Amendments proposed by one Legislature would lie over until the next Legislature in order that the newspapers might lay them before the people. In this way the people can express their opinions more directly as to the fundamental law of the state. Give the people a chance to say whether or not they would like this plan. It is the duty of this Council to lay this before the people for their verdict. The minority of this committee feel that this action is demanded by the people.

On the afternoon of Tuesday, August 3, Judge H. Henry Powers for the majority of the committee made a supplementary report to this effect. (¹) "Our Constitution was framed for the *whole* people." It does not govern municipalities but the people; it should be controlled by the people, and the municipalities ought not to control it. The Council of Censors is elected by the *people* on a general ticket. (²) "Theoretically, then, the Council created by the people themselves more emphatically represents the popular voice than any other tribunal in our frame of government." Evidently this was the purpose of the framers of the Constitution when they established the Council. It would have been better to submit amendments to a Convention representing the people not the towns; but this was not the case.

(¹) Journal of 1869, p. 70.
(²) Journal of 1869, p. 71.

Delegates to Constitutional Conventions have been chosen by towns. A town with fifty voters can thus have a voice in determining the organic law of the state equal to that of Rutland with fifteen hundred or two thousand voters. (¹) This is not right or just. An amendment to change the method of calling Constitutional Conventions so as to represent the whole people would bring the people nearer to a direct participation in amending the Constitution, than the plan proposed by the minority report. As the Senate is now made up it represents the idea of municipality because each county, whatever its size, has one at least (the other sixteen being given to the larger counties on the basis of population) and the House represents the towns as corporations regardless of population; and yet the minority of this committee recommend the placing of the initiative of amendment with the Legislature thus made, as being nearer the people. What matters it if other states have not employed it; or, if they have used it and then discarded it? Vermont has other institutions not possessed by other states; but this is no argument why she should discard them. "The very *soul* of an organic law—of a constitution for a commonwealth, is *permanency*." (²) The people demand a permanent law as a protection for their rights.

On the ground of economy, a Council of Censors once in seven years, followed by a Constitutional Convention, would prove, he believed, every whit as economical as the method proposed by the minority. If the Legislature can propose amendments once in ten years "a large portion of their time will be spent in tinkering it." The Constitution will then be a target for repeated blows by the members of the Legislature; and all this will be expensive. The people do not desire to confer upon the Legislature the other powers held by the Council of Censors, then why give up this one?

(¹) Journal of Censors, 1869, p. 71.
(²) Journal of Censors, 1869, p. 72.

Several efforts have been made in the past to do away with the Council of Censors, but they have not met with success, "and although in deference to the wishes of a portion of our people who call for this change we may be constrained to vote to submit the proposed amendment of the minority to a convention, still in justice to ourselves we are bound to express our views against the wisdom of such a change". (¹)

On October 22, 1869, the Council of Censors voted to present a series of proposed amendments to be acted on by a convention duly elected by the people, the substance of which was: (1) That the Council of Censors should be abolished, and that the Legislature should, once in ten years, have the right to initiate amendments to the Constitution; (2) no special laws for corporations except for municipal purposes; (3) State officers in all departments to be elected biennially; (4) senators and town representatives to be elected for two years; (5) judges of the Supreme Court to be appointed by the Governor, " by and with the advice and consent of the Senate." The term of office of judges should be six years, and they should be divided into classes, the term of office of one-third expiring every two years. The salaries should not be diminished during the term of office. But if the above, relative to election of judges, should fail of ratification, then it was proposed, as a substitute, that they should be elected biennally and that their term of office should be two years; (6) women to have no more restrictions than men in regard to voting.

The Council of Censors, October 19, 1869, voted to call a Constitutional Convention to meet at Montpelier, Vt., the second Wednesday in June, 1870, " to consider certain amendments to the Constitution of this State proposed by the Council of Censors."

The Convention met according to the call of the Censors and proceeded to consider the amendments proposed.

(¹) Journal of 1869, p. 72.

It is curious to note the spirit of the Convention as manifested in the vote on the different articles. That suggesting biennial sessions of the Legislature was carried by a majority of five votes out of a total of 233; that making the term of judges of the Supreme Court six years was defeated by a majority of two hundred and twenty-nine out of a total vote of two hundred and thirty-one, but two votes being cast in its favor. The amendment proposing woman suffrage received but one vote in its favor, while two hundred and thirty-three were cast against it. The article abolishing the Council of Censors and giving the power to the Legislature to take the initiative in amending the Constitution, and this once in ten years, was carried by a vote of one hundred and twenty-three in its favor and eighty-five against the measure,—not a two-thirds vote.

General Comment.

At the February session of the Legislature, 1779, an act was passed declaring that the Constitution as established by general convention at Windsor, in 1777, with the alterations made agreeably to Section 44 of the Constitution " shall be forever considered, held and maintained, as part of the laws of this State."(1)

A similar act was passed at Windsor at the June session of 1782 " to prevent disputes respecting the legal (2) force of the Constitution of this State " and(3) again in 1787. In these two acts the Constitution is treated as if it were a legislative act in point of quality.

Judge Chipman in his *Memoirs of Thomas Chittenden*(4) shows that the early people of Vermont, in common with many others, held that sovereignty was vested in the

(1) Slade, State Papers, p. 288.
(2) Slade, State Papers, p. 449.
(3) Memoirs of Thomas Chittenden, p. 111.
(4) P. 102.

Legislature, or in the people, but manifested in the action of the Legislature. From this it would follow that a Constitution would stand only on an equal footing with acts of the Legislature. This view changed when the Constitution of the United States was adopted as the supreme law of the land.

In a previous dissertation we have shown the origin of the Council of Censors, as having some features analogous to the Greek ephors; that it had some features like those of the Roman Censors, whence it took its name; that it was a feature of Rousseau's *Social Contract;* that in the republics of France and Naples, at one time, it was proposed seriously as the people's check on the usurpations of the various departments of government. The Radicals of Pennsylvania adopted it in the Constitution of that State in 1776, and discarded it in the Constitution of 1790. In Pennsylvania only one Council of Censors was ever elected and this body by a majority vote favored submitting a proposition for amending the Constitution by abolishing this provision. A two-thirds vote was needed to carry this, hence it was never submitted as an amendment.

Vermont adopted this provision with the entire Pennsylvania Constitution, with certain minor changes, in 1777. Fourteen times at intervals of seven years, Councils of Censors were elected, and nine Constitutional Conventions were called to consider proposed amendments. Finally in 1870 it was abolished and the initiative for amending the Constitution was vested in the Legislature, the power to be active only once in ten years. Judge Chipman in his *Memoirs of Thomas Chittenden* (¹) says that the Vermont Council of Censors being elected on a general ticket, this threw the advantage into the hands of the dominant party, and that by this means the minority was not represented in

(¹) P. 129.

the Council. The Censors, elected by a majority of the electors, would meet, consider the defects of the Constitution, and possibly suggest remedies; in which case it would call a Constitutional Convention. These Conventions were, except in one instance, 1857, made of delegates, one from each town. As the recommendations of the Censors were placed before the people before the delegates to the Constitutional Convention were elected, the minority party would succeed in sending, in most cases, a majority of delegates opposed to the provisions of the Censors. The Councils of Censors were, then, radical or progressive, while the Conventions were conservative.

From 1793 to 1836 only one amendment was ratified by a Constitutional Convention, and this denied the right of suffrage to all foreign-born citizens until they should be naturalized. In 1836, the amendment to make the legislature bi-cameral passed by a majority of only three votes, one hundred and sixteen votes being cast in favor of the measure and one hundred and thirteen against. Successive Councils of Censors had three times previously recommended this change but it had always been rejected, although Vermont was the only state in the Union having a legislature of only one branch.

The spirit of progress and conservatism in the Censors on the one hand and the Conventions on the other, is illustrated by the attempts made to lengthen the term of the supreme court judges. Five times was the effort made and five times the measure was defeated. This was begun in 1814, was repeated in 1822, 1857 and 1870, when it received the crushing defeat of two votes for the measure, and two hundred and thirty-one votes against it. Thus have the people kept a strong grasp on the judiciary, calling upon the bench to give an account of its stewardship before the bar of each biennial Legislature.

Perhaps the greatest controversy between the Censors and the Conventions occurred in connection with the recommendations of the Council of 1856. That body prepared a series of amendments, among them the provision for biennial sessions of the Legislature, with provision for two-year periods for State officials, and then issued a call for a Constitutional Convention of ninety members, apportioned among the counties, " in such manner as will, in our opinion,(¹) protect the just rights of all." The *Address* further stated, "And we submit to you whether the principle on which said Convention is based is not under existing institutions in accordance with your views of right, in matters relating to the fundamental and organic Laws of the State."

The Convention of 1857 met and organized. A committee of one from each county was appointed to decide upon a course of action with reference to the proposed amendments, with Paul Dillingham as chairman. His report recited that the amendments were numerous and important, that they contemplated many and radical changes in our Constitution. The committee declined to give an opinion as to merits or demerits of the amendments. It regarded the plan of limiting the delegates to ninety, and apportioned as they were, as a startling innovation. The committee reviewed the framing and amending that had been done since 1777, and called attention to the statement in the preamble of the instrument, that it should be permanent and unchanged, until it should be changed in a manner provided by the express terms of the instrument. The Convention expressed its views to the people in four resolutions to the effect (1) that the Censors had acted unwisely in thus calling a Convention; (2) that in the absence of precise words, the practice and usage of many years had confirmed the purpose of the fathers to establish town representation in Conventions, which purpose it urged the next Legislature to confirm explicitly; (3) that, because these delegates did not represent the towns, they were

---

(¹) Address of Council of Censors, 1856, p. 108.

chosen by their constituencies to reprobate the action of the Censors, not to give validity to their action; and (4) that as this Convention was not duly constituted as prescribed by time-honored usage and custom it would take no further action. It adjourned and thus referred the points at issue to the judgment of the people.

In these collisions between the progressive spirit of the able men who set on foot progressive movements in governmental matters, and the conservative spirit of the people in the Constitutional Conventions, one sees an example of the working of the referendum. The experience of Vermont has been repeated in Switzerland since 1874. Sir Henry Maine says, ([1]) "Contrary to all expectations, to the bitter disappointment of the authors of the Referendum, laws of the highest importance, some of them openly framed for popularity, have been vetoed by the people after they had been adopted by the Federal or Cantonal Legislature."

The Convention of 1870 was made up of delegates from each town and, hence, was duly constituted. Its cautious work is in evidence when one considers that the matter of biennial sessions of the legislature was carried by a majority of only five votes out of two hundred and thirty-three; that the proposition granting the right of suffrage to women received only one vote in its favor to two hundred and thirty-three in opposition; and that the Council of Censors was abolished and the method of taking the initiative in amending the Constitution was lodged in the Legislature by a majority of only thirty-eight out of a vote of two hundred and eight.

([1]) Popular Government, pp. 96-7.